Introduction to Revenue Management for Hotels

Tools and strategies to maximize the revenue of your property

D1731510

Gemma Hereter

ISBN: **1542609054**
ISBN-13: **978-1542609050**

THE REASON FOR THIS BOOK

Welcome to the exciting world of Revenue Management! You've probably been looking for a book that would introduce you to this little-known world and this new kind of career.

There are not many books or courses out there about this topic, and the ones that have been written are too tough or deep and do not give you an introduction to this complex profession.

Being a Revenue Manager myself and having worked in different departments in different hotel chains, I decided to put into words all that I have learned during the years and explain what Revenue Managers do in their everyday work.

You are about to get to know not only the basics and concepts of revenue management, but also techniques and different ways to apply it to different departments.

The desire to offer my vision and knowledge on this subject gave me the motivation to write this book and I hope you enjoy it as much as I have enjoyed writing it. The first step is to invite you to connect on social networks such as LinkedIn, because this is a great tool to get referrals, job offers, promotions and to be in touch for future questions that you might have. If you don't have a LinkedIn account yet, I would like to encourage you to create one, as it is a great tool for professionals. You can check out my profile in Linkedin, send me an invitation and I will be happy to add you to my circle of contacts!

WHY YOU SHOULD READ THIS BOOK

In this book, we will not only talk about Revenue Management, but also about the importance of social networks and brand and online reputation; this is not a book just focused on Revenue Management.

I have worked as a freelance marketing manager and I take brand reputation very seriously. I believe in the potential of brand awareness in companies and hotels and the direct impact that it has on their revenue.

What will we cover in this book?

- What is Revenue Management

- The fundamentals of Revenue Management

- The main implementation strategies

-Which organizational steps have to be implemented and what Revenue Management strategy steps.

- Analysis

- Forecast

- Pricing

- Benchmarking

- Channel management

- Dumping

- Hotel online marketing

- Online reputation

- And the salaries offered for this position in the world :)

All these topics will be covered with examples, which will make the reading more dynamic and agile.

So, let's get started on this passionate topic!

TABLE OF CONTENTS

WHO SHOULD READ THIS BOOK

This book is addressed to professionals who are related to the accommodation industry, or to any student or anyone who is working at a hotel, restaurant, hostel or apartments and who is interested in Revenue Management.

I studied tourism and then took a postgraduate degree in Event and Hotel Management. Of course at that time, thirteen or fourteen years ago, there wasn't a subject of Revenue Management at the University. Nowadays there are postgraduate educations, masters and many types of courses to do after college.

If you work at a convention department or reception, or you are a concierge or a hotel manager, you should have at least an introduction to Revenue Management because, as you will see in this book, any person working at a hotel is as important as the Revenue Manager his or herself. This is because, at the end of the day, with your daily and maybe minor decisions, you are also engaged in revenue management - this department is not a department of one person, but requires the involvement of the whole hotel. That's why I think that if you work, or would like to work, in the hotel industry this book is for you.

This book is also for Revenue Managers, and for workers and managers of golf clubs, bars, restaurants, and cinemas; in fact, all those companies that may be able to generate more revenue through a good application of Revenue Management.

SECTION 1. FUNDAMENTALS OF REVENUE MANAGEMENT

INTRODUCTION

The first step for a revenue manager to make decisions on pricing and its different sales strategies is to collect data, aggregate it, analyze it, and then forecast both the demand and performance. Once that is done, it is time to make informed decisions and put them in place through the various channels. In simplified terms what a Revenue Manager does is **understand, anticipate, and react to market demand in order to maximize revenues.**

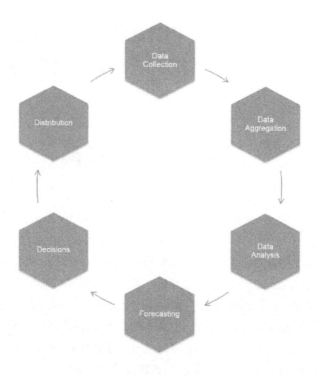

Image by Snapshot.travel

1. WHAT IS REVENUE MANAGEMENT

Revenue Management has its beginnings in **Yield Management,** which was born in the airline industry in the seventies. This arose because there was an American airline that was launched suddenly and set its prices quite low. Nowadays we would call this company a 'low-cost' company. Because of the competition, another airline company that already existed also decided to put down its prices - but also started to sell airline tickets to the top class customers willing to pay a higher price. What happened? The company that used Yield Management survived and the other went bankrupt - that was the beginning of Yield Management.

What is Revenue Management? ***Revenue Management is the technique used to sell the right product at the right time to the right customer at the right price.*** We will see a little more specifically what is the right thing that we need to sell, at what price, to whom and at what time. As I said, there is a difference between Yield and Revenue Management.

Revenue Management is based on the economic theory of supply and demand - you alter your rates so that you can get more incremental revenue, because different guests are willing to pay a different price for using the same amount of resources.[1]

- **Right customer**

The 'right' customer is a debatable concept from a marketing point of view but could be associated with the target market segment which has been identified by the hotel's marketing manager and whose requirements are taken into consideration when preparing the product of the hotel. The concept of the 'right' customer calls for the hotel to use various marketing techniques in order to attract the customers which it could properly and profitable serve and deny accommodation for the rest. Hotels, for example, put minimum stay requirements during specific busy periods (e.g. during fairs, exhibitions, world championships) so that they dissuade transit one-night stays in favour of more profitable longer stay customers.

---

[1] (Stanislav Ivanov (2014). Hotel Revenue Management: From Theory to Practice. Varna: Zangador.)

8

- **Right Product**

The right product is determined by both the customers and the hoteliers. It is the product that a) delivers value to the 'right' customers by satisfying their needs, wants, requirements, b) reflects the customer's willingness to pay, and c) is profitable for the hotelier. It is useless to offer services and amenities in the hotel that do not fit the requirements of the target market segment, or offer services/amenities which these customers could not afford to buy or the hotel cannot provide profitably.

- **Right distribution channel**

The hotel can sell its product via various distribution channels. It could sell directly to the customers or via travel agencies [tour operators and travel agents, or online travel agencies (OTAs)], global distribution systems (GDSs), online reservation systems, etc. (Ivanov & Zhechev, 2011). Each distribution channel provides access to different customers and requires different costs to sustain. Therefore, from the perspective of the revenue management's goal, the 'right' distribution channel is the channel that provides access to the 'right' customer and is cost effective to sustain.

- **Right price**

The price is one of the most important instruments in the arsenal of revenue management tools because it is directly linked with the level of the revenues. By changing the level of prices over time, the ratio between different prices for various market segments (the so called "price structure") and the conditions applicable for each price level the hotel can attract the 'right' customers and generate high revenues. The 'right' price is the price that the customer is willing to pay and the hotel is willing to charge. Obviously the customers would like to pay as little as possible, while the hotels would prefer to charge as much as possible. However, if the customer feels that he has been overcharged and the price paid does not reflect the value received from the product, then future relationships between both parties are at stake.

- **Right time**

Timing is one of the most significant concepts in revenue management. One and the same offer could be perceived differently only on the basis of when it has been made. A pre-Christmas stay promotion offered in July would most probably remain unnoticed because it is published too early. The same offer at the beginning of December might also be inefficient because it could be too late for the customers to make bookings at the hotel to use the promotion. The right time would depend on the booking patterns of the different market segments. If the target segment usually makes most of the bookings within two weeks before the check-in date, then the optimum date for the release of the promotion might be 2-3 weeks before check-in in order for the promotion to be noticed by the potential customers.

- **Right communication**

In the context of revenue management, marketing communications of the hotel influence how its product and prices are perceived. The way information is provided on the hotel's website or how prices are presented can influence customers' perceptions about the value they receive from consuming the hotel's product, and the fairness of the price conditions. This impacts the perceived 'price/value' ratio and customers' satisfaction from the purchase and their future purchase intentions.

Differences between yield and revenue management

Yield management is a variable pricing strategy, based on understanding, anticipating and influencing consumer behavior in order to maximize revenue or profits from a fixed, time-limited resource (such as airline seats or hotel room reservations or advertising inventory). As a specific, inventory-focused branch of revenue management, yield management involves strategic control of inventory to sell it to the right customer at the right time for the right price. This process can result in price discrimination, in which customers consuming identical goods or services are charged different prices. Yield management is a large revenue generator for several major industries. Robert Crandall, former Chairman and CEO of American

Airlines, gave yield management its name and has called it "the single most important technical development in transportation management since we entered deregulation."

So, whereas the Yield was born in the American airlines in the seventies, the Revenue was born with the evolution of Yield Management.

Yield Management optimizes the income per flown mile per passenger and the percentage of seats that have been sold - it is basically centered on the achievement of maximum income; the difference with Revenue is that Revenue Management is focused on a daily effort to increase *RevPAR*.

RevPAR is the Revenue per Available Room, and the trick is to find a balance between occupation and the average price; this is the main difference between Yield and Revenue.

Currently, hotels make Revenue and airlines have evolved and make Revenue as well, but airlines basically do Yield Management.

2. WHY IS REVENUE MANAGEMENT USED AT HOTELS

As you will know, a hotel's inventory is *perishable*; that means that a room that is not sold today at price x, cannot be sold tomorrow, because that day is gone. You will not be able to sell that room at a higher price today if you didn't sell it yesterday, because you cannot simply add that amount to today's product; that's why we should always try to sell as many rooms as possible at the right price every day. Therefore, the hotelier tries to manage the demand through various tools to try to switch the demand from busy periods to other less busy periods. It is our task to try to **get the maximum revenue per sold room.** Customers would look for tangible clues about the quality of the product – hotel descriptions, pictures, guest reviews, which increases the role of marketing communication in the presentation of hotel's product value.

What is the situation with a hotel? A hotel has got a **fixed room capacity**, let's say, for example, a hundred rooms per day to sell. We know that we will have bookings that have booked in advance, *expected arrivals* and we also have a number of rooms or reservations that customers book on the same day of the arrival (*unexpected arrivals*). In addition, the hotels have a variable demand depending on the period (seasons, events, fairs, etc.).

For example, a hotel by the beach where the seasonality is very high (usually in the summer) or one at the mountains which will have a high season in winter, during the ski period, are not the same. That is why demand is highly variable over time - we must plan and anticipate the periods of high and low demand.

Besides room capacity, we can identify capacities for the various other revenue generating services such as restaurant, meeting rooms, spa centre, sauna... These capacities are determined in a similar manner as the room capacity – the number of customers that could be served within a specific time period, e.g. number of customers that could take massage in one day. Similar to room capacity, the capacities of the restaurant, the spa centre, the sauna, etc., would depend on the number seats or deck chairs. However, besides the pure physical limitations, the capacity of these revenue centres of the hotel would also be influenced by other factors such as personnel etc.[2]

What else does a hotel have? A hotel has got **fixed costs**, which are those costs that will have to be paid even if the hotel is full or empty. Some examples of a fixed cost would be the rent, the personnel's wages, or the water or electricity supply bills. This means that you have to know what the fixed cost per room is that your hotel has, so that you know at least the minimum price you need to cover those costs when selling that room.

There's also the **market segmentation**, which we will discuss in further chapters; this will help us to know where our customers come from and in which periods - with this it will be easy to predict the occupation depending on the seasonality and by market.

Revenue Management can also be applied in other businesses, such as bars, restaurants, fitness clubs, etc. Why could it be applied in other businesses, such as restaurants? Because in the case of a restaurant, for

---

[2] (Stanislav Ivanov (2014). *Hotel Revenue Management: From Theory to Practice*)

example, you may have products that are perishable and are going to expire in a short period of time. It might be good management to promote that you are selling those products at a special price, otherwise, money will be lost (i.e. the product cost). It may also a good idea, for example, to have promotions on drinks or menus - with a big discount on days or at hours that the business is quieter. The goal is to attract customers with offers and fill the bar or the restaurant, with the intention that the customers stay after the 'happy hour' and keep on buying other drinks or dishes that don't have a discount.

Likewise, revenue management can be applied in cinemas and theaters. At the cinemas, there are a certain days or sessions that the cinema might be empty or not that busy.

To apply revenue management in other businesses we:

1. Manage profitability:

- Make a monthly and annual budget

- Know the balance point of the business

- Perform the income statement

- Check sales

- Control costs

2. Manage costs:

- Calculate the cost of the dishes (bar, restaurant)

- Conduct inventory of goods

- Monitor regularly the purchasing costs

- Calculate the food cost in the restaurant

- Calculate food expirations

3. Manage sales:

- Know the average ticket per person of your business (what is spent on average per person)

- Know what the average consumer ticket is at key times (morning, afternoon, evening, weekend ...)

- Know the consumption number of customers per day and time

- Know the gross margin contributed by each product or service

4. Marketing Management:

- Conduct sales promotions

- Have indicators of customer satisfaction

- Know your competitors

- Make upselling in your business

- Launch new products periodically

- Advertise and promote your business

Actions we can take:

- Varying consumer prices during the week and by the time of consumption

- Tell the staff what dishes / products / movies etc. should be sold and given priority.

3. APPLYING REVENUE MANAGEMENT

AT HOTELS

Which analytical tools can be applied when conducting Revenue Management?

- Market segmentation

- Analysing past and future trends

- Forecasts

- Pricing strategies

- Overbooking strategies

How do we apply Revenue Management? We need to know the **market segmentation.** It is very important to know what type of market segment comes to our hotel, and whether most of your guests booked from tour operators, and whether they come for leisure, business, business groups, conventions, meetings... We will have to analyze the past using the historical bookings, and its prices as well as the total production. Along with all this, we have to apply a pricing strategy in the current

19

year watching the competition and the annual budget, which usually will have been approved by the hotel manager, Director of Revenue or any other Commercial Director.

We will have to make a **strategy of overbooking** because we all know that although we are full on a particular date, there are x number of reservations that are cancelled, either because they are no-show or because some travellers may cancel their bookings some days before the arrival or on the same day, depending on the restrictions applied to each booking. We will have to prepare a Forecast Demand, to predict the demand in the future.

Usually this forecast is 3 months ahead, giving you the tools to predict the occupation and rates and to act if things are not going as predicted on the budget.

4. MARKET SEGMENTATION

Regarding the market segmentation, we will make a **pricing segmentation** - this means that we will set a price for each market segment. We will analyze the turnover of each market segment and the revenue that they can bring to our hotel.

For example, if we are a hotel that is located in a business area, then certainly an important segment will be the business one. We must set a price forecast and analyze when the demand can be higher and the amount of room nights or percentage that this segment represents for our hotel. This will help us to segment each type of market and predict our demand.

Types of segments that a hotel could have:

- **Leisure segment,** includes *individual leisure,* for example the type of customers who come for leisure to a city or a tourist destination, cruise customers, customers who come with packages (flight + hotel). We can identify those who come with a range of services included.

Within the leisure segment we can differentiate into *groups of leisure,* when we have requests from groups, tour groups, *and series of circuits.*

- **Business Segment,** differentiating amongst *companies, business groups, conferences, incentives, meetings,* etc.

In order to segment your customers, the booking department of your hotel must introduce the booking into your system correctly (if your system allows you to introduce the different segments) and the booking agents or those who are in charge of introducing the bookings should know for each booking to which segment those clients belong. Sometimes it's not easy to know the reason for the stay of some of the customers; for example, they might be booking through Expedia or Booking.com but coming for business purposes - in this case, the reception department should try to guess or find out the reason for the stay of that customer and if needed modify the reservation in the hotel's booking system. This will help us to prepare the budget correctly in the following years because we will have detected the segments of our customers and the average price that they are paying. Additionally, for sales and commercial purposes, it will be very useful to get as much data and information from the customer as possible, such as email, phone number, preferences during his/her stay, etc. We will then be able to offer him/her the best competitive rate to book directly with the hotel and not through an online agency, because of the commissions and the more personalized treatment that we can give to our guests.

5. MEASURE OF REVENUE

How can we measure the efficiency of our income and the technique used for Revenue Management? What indicators indicate revenue? How can we measure the revenue in our hotel?

There are some hotels and hotel chains that **only** consider the **occupation rate** as an indicator of success or failure in assessing how the business is progressing, but this indicator is not good enough and not totally valid to measure the revenue of a property; in my view, it is not a good way of managing a business.

We have several indicators that provide us with various data. Amongst them, the one that is gaining more importance lately is the **RevPAR;** the RevPAR is the revenue per available room. From my point of view I think it is one of the best indicators.

For example, if your hotel has got 100 rooms and January has got 31 days, this means that in January we can sell 3.100 rooms. If we have a production of 98.000 Euros, that means that our RevPAR is €31,61.

 100 rooms x 31 days = 3.100 rooms available to sell a month.

€98.000 income / 3.100 rooms = €31,61

If we made a comparison with the previous years, it would be a good thing that this indicator would go up, not down. It would indicate to us that, with the same amount of available rooms, we have a higher income.

Another indicator is the **ADR,** which is the Average Daily Rate or the average price of a sold room per day; this indicator shows us at what price we are selling each occupied room. For example, if in January we sold 1.550 rooms and have produced 98.000 Euros, our average price in January was €63,22. This indicator can also be used to compare the price of that particular month with the same month in previous years.

We can have monthly average prices and yearly average prices.

Some of the other indicators are:

Trevpar: Total revenue per available room.

GopPar: profit per available room.

Revpam: conference and banqueting revenue per available square meter.

Revpash: food and beverage revenue per available seat and hour.

6. APPLYING STRATEGIES

There are some strategies that can be applied in order to have a higher profit and benefit in revenue in our property.

One of them is **availability management;** we must know at all times how many rooms are available to be sold at the property and we have to do our best to promote the selling of those rooms; we also need to know how to manage the **overbooking** very well. Although this word might sound to you like *'danger! danger!'*, in fact most revenue managers and hotel managers love the words: *we have overbooking.* A good way to make revenue is to practice overbooking; this doesn't mean overbooking of 10 or 20 rooms, but only a few, considering that x number of rooms tend to be *no-show* or canceled at a very short notice; we can experience the fact of being fully booked for a particular day and all of a sudden to have some rooms that need to be sold.

Rooms are a perishable product that if we don't sell on a particular day we will not be able to sell them on the following day, as that day is gone. We must try to sell, at the best price, the maximum amount of rooms per day.

I'm not a huge fan of overbooking, but we should have the option to be able to send those overbooked rooms to another hotel.

We also need to apply properly CTA (**close out day**) - the **minimum length of stay** and the **maximum length of stay.** Those are strategies that are used when forcing customers to stay a minimum or a maximum number of nights. This is especially useful if there are some special events, bank holidays or high demand dates. It would also be a good strategy to ask for a minimum length of stay for large groups or groups of rooms that are willing to book, for instance, at weekends (if your occupation rate is higher at the weekends) and forcing them to stay on Friday and Saturday night or applying a certain discount if they stay for a 2 or 3-night minimum.

7. INVENTORY VS REVENUE

MANAGEMENT

What are the differences between Inventory and Revenue Management?

The goal of **Inventory Management** is to sell all rooms; and the goal of Revenue Management is to sell those rooms, but at the best price. Inventory Management tries to optimize space, for example, also selling meeting rooms, restaurant services, etc., considering the sales restrictions as well as the types of rooms for sale. No pricing, cross-selling or upselling is done.

Revenue Management aims to sell those rooms at the best price considering the rise and fall of prices of the competitors and the demand. It is not the same to sell a room at 80€ that one at 90€, because we could have sold the right room to the right person at the right time.

8. UNLIMITED DEMAND

The **unlimited demand** or **unconstrained demand** is the complete demand that we could have in a day. For example, in a period of high demand, such as a weekend, if we have many requests from groups plus individual sales, and we have 100 rooms booked and we are fully booked, the unlimited or complete demand is the booked rooms plus the rejected rooms, the no show and the cancelled rooms. Thus, we have to calculate the maximum capacity that the hotel might have had and at what price we could have sold it; instead of selling each room at €80 per night, maybe we could have sold it for €90 or €95.

This will help us to make a more precise forecast for the forthcoming years so that we can predict at what price we could have sold every room in that particular period.

Day	OTB	1	2	3	4	5	6	7	8	9	10
Segment 1	Room nigths	23	25	19	33	33	19	17	15	10	5
	Pick up Exp	3	5	10	11	12	15	17	23	25	30
Segment 2	Room nigths	12	13	10	17	17	10	9	8	5	3
	Pick up Exp	7	9	14	15	16	19	21	27	29	34
Segment 3	Room nigths	27	29	23	37	37	23	21	19	14	9
	Pick up Exp	5	7	12	13	14	17	19	25	27	32
Total Bookings		77	88	88	126	129	103	104	117	110	113
Number of Hotel Rooms		100	100	100	100	100	100	100	100	100	100
Exceeding demand		0	0	0	26	29	3	4	17	10	13

Exercise: Prepare an Excel document that includes the details of bookings, dates of booking, check ins and petitions that you have, and also include the cancellations, the length of stays, market segments and the total amount of revenue earnt.

Prepare another Excel document which includes the hotel cancellations and the clients cancellations, in order to be able to follow up the requests made, to be able to predict future demand and to get to know the reasons why some bookings were not confirmed.

9. NECESSARY STEPS

What are the necessary steps to implement a good Revenue Management strategy? First of all, the Revenue Manager has to **involve the entire sales team, management and reception team** to work with him; that means explaining to the team and putting them in the situation of the person in charge of the Revenue Management of the hotel. This person has to make all of all the other staff of the hotel, especially those who are involved in sales and with the upselling and cross-selling (bar, restaurant, reception, spa team...), knowledgeable about the sales strategy and objectives that the property needs to reach and accomplish. This strategy is not the work of one person, but is the work of a whole team, although in most cases it is developed by only one person. That means that although we have one person in charge of making the strategy of Revenue Management, there will be other departments, such as the reservations, sales or groups departments, that depend on the strategy and implementation of the prices that the Revenue Manager will create. So it is very important that the whole team gets involved and knows at all times where the hotel is driving to and what objectives and strategies need to be followed. It is important to have at least a weekly meeting with the entire team (hotel manager, sales manager, head of reception ...) so that everyone knows at all times the strategies that have to be applied and the decisions that have been taken.

10. ANALYSIS

To apply a good Revenue strategy, the revenue team has got to analyze the situation. The data to be analyzed includes the following:

☐Average daily rate

☐Occupation

☐RevPar

☐Pick Up

☐Length of stay

☐ Geographical Origin

☐Segments

The revenue team or Revenue Manager will have to analyze the **daily, monthly and yearly average rate.** First of all, the room's revenue budget will have to be as realistic as possible and it will have to be analyzed daily, weekly and monthly to determine if the evolution of the revenue and average rate is the desired one.

The same must be applied to the **RevPAR;** we will also analyze what is the daily and monthly **pick up,** (the volume of bookings that are done daily or monthly), how it is evolving compared to previous years and what can be done to improve it. The pick up can be analyzed by segments or in a more generic way. Also the **segments** and how are they evolving will have to be analyzed.

We will also analyze the **length of stay** of our customers because it may vary from one year to another or it might depend on certain factors such as the geographical origin of the customer. The length of stay might vary according to nationality as someone from a country further away than others will probably stay longer and someone with a closer nationality will perhaps stay for fewer days.

How do we analyze this? With reports from our system. It will depend on the kind of system or program that we are using whether we will be able to get more or less detailed reports, and we might not be able to get all the data that we need. What will we analyze with the data? We will need to analyze the historical data, from the past, and present data. Of course we will need to consider the future, especially to check and forecast the following months. All this will help us to undertake a study of the income that we will have at the hotel.

SECTION 2. THE TOOLS

11. THE BUDGET

What are the tools that a Revenue Manager uses to analyze the situation of the hotel and how to reach its objective? The first thing that the Revenue Manager has to do with the sales or commercial team is to prepare the **budget.**

The budget has to be divided by departments (rooms, restaurant, spa, etc.) and there has to be a global budget - a sum-up that includes the entire budget of the hotel. This budget must be broken down on a monthly basis and encompassed in the annual budget.

The budget shows us in a quantitative way the objectives that need to be achieved in a hotel; it will reflect the costs, purchases, sales ... everything that needs to be known at the end of the year.

What are the advantages of having a budget? The budget will give us a **clear objective** and we will become focused on it. It will allow us to **increase the control over each ratio and control the results**. It will allow us to set priorities; for example, if in a particular month the department of Food and Beverage is not evolving as it should be as per budget, it will be the right time to take actions in order to reach the budget at year-end or at the end of the semester by having positive results during the same month. Thanks to the analysis of that budget, those responsible for each department will have the tools to measure the success or the failure of their departments and will be able to anticipate them.

Basically, to develop a budget we must follow five steps:

1 – Revenue

We have to review our revenues from the past year and make a statement of the estimated revenue we can generate in the following year, the one we are quoting.

The revenue (in the case of accommodation) is the product of two variables: **the occupancy** in the form of room nights and the **average price** or ADR (Average Daily Rate) of the room.

We can generate two type of incomes: one where we are told about what growth is expected, for example a total of 4%. So, in that case we will disaggregate into a 0,71% increase in ADR and 3,26% in occupancy. And we adjust it by segments (or inverted in order to balance it) or by sales/distribution channels.

Hotel Barcelona 4*			Rooms	100 rooms			
			Nights	365 days			
			available RN	36500			

	2019				Budget 2020			
Segments	Room nights	%	ADR	Revenue	Room nights	%	ADR	Revenue
BAR	15.695	43%	95,3	1.495.733,50	16.000	44	96,55	1.544.800
TTOO	1.825	5%	82,7	150.927,50	1.845	5	85,25	157.286
Promotional	2.190	6%	98,25	215.167,50	2.295	6	98,35	225.713
Corporate	5.475	15%	93,1	509.722,50	5.750	16	93,5	537.625
Groups	3.625	10%	85,3	309.212,50	3.860	11	87,086	336.152
TOTAL	28.810	79%	93,04	2.680.763,50	29750	82	94,17	2.801.576
					3,26%		0,71%	

In the above table we can see 2019´s closure by segments (BAR, the promotional rate, TTOO, corporate and groups) with the room nights and ADR or PM; and for the 2020´s budget we can see that we have increased the revenue by 3,26% and the occupancy by 0,71%.

In the next table we will project a revenue forecast for 2020, breaking it down into each month.

CIERRE 2019	ENE	FEB	MAR	ABR*	MAY
DIAS/MES	31	28	31	30	31
HABITACIONES	100	100	100	100	100
ROOM NIGHTS DISPONIBLES	3.100	2.800	3.100	3.000	3.100
OCUPACIÓN	1.994	2.331	2.571	2.379	2.691
OCC%	64%	83%	83%	79%	87%
ADR	85,6 €	95,4 €	96,7 €	93,5 €	98,1 €
TOTAL ROOM REVENUE	170.686 €	222.377 €	248.616 €	222.437 €	263.987 €

PRESUPUESTO 2020	ENE	FEB	MAR*	ABR	MAY
DIAS/MES	31	29	31	30	31
HABITACIONES	100	100	100	100	100
ROOM NIGHTS DISPONIBLES	3.100	2.900	3.100	3.000	3.100
OCUPACIÓN INCREMENTO LINEAL	2.059	2.407	2.655	2.457	2.779
AJUSTE MANUAL OCUPACIÓN	2.059	2.407	2.450	2.650	2.739
OCC%	66%	83%	79%	88%	88%
ADR	86,2 €	96,1 €	97,4 €	94,2 €	98,8 €
ADR AJUSTE MANUAL ADR	86,2 €	96,1 €	93,3 €	96,0 €	101,0 €
TOTAL ROOM REVENUE	177.514 €	231.273 €	258.560 €	231.334 €	274.547 €
TOTAL ROOM REVENUE AJUSTADO	177.514 €	231.272 €	228.585 €	254.400 €	276.639 €

MAR* ABR* INCLUYE SEMANA SANTA

2 –Costs

- **The Fixed Costs** are produced one way or

another; they are the hotel rent or mortgage, one part of the staff (the management team, maintenance, reception, reservation, insurance...)

- **The Variable Costs** are produced for each one of the sold/occupied room as the cleaning of the room if it is outsourced, of the bedding...

An example of a cost for a double room would be:

- Outsource cleaning cost: 5€

- Laundry cost: 2€

- Amenities cost: 0,45€

- Paper cost + check in-out: 0,1 €

- Water: 0,1€

- Energy: 1€

Total: 8,65€

- **The Semi-variable Costs** as investment cost for marketing, electricity, water, heating...

The **contribution margin** is the difference between what we pay for the room minus variable costs, which is what it contributes, first to cover fixed costs and then to become a profit.

Revenue 100€

Variable Costs 40€

Contribution Margin 60€

The selling price of our rooms must be higher than the variable costs, otherwise we would be paying the clients to come to our hotel.

This 60€ of Contribution Margin will cover the fixed costs and the profit.

The **Impasse** is the moment in which the hotel starts generating profits. The Revenues of the rooms contribute to pay the variable costs, in the first place, and then to continue paying the fixed costs, which is the moment we reach the Impasse.

The Impasse is the level of sales in which the contribution margin covers the fixed costs. For example:

Impasse 45.000€/60€ = 750

Room Nights

750 RNs for 30 nights= 25 rooms/night

Thus, starting from an occupancy of 25 rooms per night, our hotel would start generating profit, due to the full cover of variable and fixes costs.

3 – Budget

To make the budget as the occupation and the average price, it has to vary from month to month; the most practical way of doing it is to budget these two variables for each of the twelve months regarding the previous year (for example, Easter may be in March one year, and the following could be in April, or the other way around, and the bank holidays vary from year to year), as well as incorporating the congresses or events that we have expected to take place and in which we predict more occupation or ADR.

4 – The Income Statement (provisional)

Now is the time to bring everything together and add the operating expenses. Many of them will be related to the turnover, and others will simply be an estimate measured in a % of the increase regarding the previous year.

5 – The Forecast

Although this phase, which is done throughout the year, is not about revenue, it is important to monitor the business development, and to forecast whether we meet the revenue, and our business goals or not.

It is important to review the forecast for each month on a weekly basis to adjust the revenue to the reality, in order to make a forecast of the variable costs (staff, electric energy, contracts, etc.) and to be as realistic as possible taking into account the revenue that was made for the current year.

12. THE RATE CALENDAR

We will have to make a **calendar** of the important events of the city or the area where our property is located. The important events can include meetings, fairs, congresses, concerts, bank holidays, conferences, arrivals of cruises, etc. These events can affect the demand in our property and because of that we will have to set special prices during them.

We call these dates **demand generators**.

We can have 4 different types of demand generators:

- **Origin Demand** generators: Some particular circumstances occur in the home market that allow clients to travel in those dates: holidays, bank holidays, the opening of new air routes, etc.

- **Destination demand** generators: Some events occur in the area where your hotel is located and it attracts travelers. Congresses, like for example the Mobile World Congress, local holidays like carnivals and concerts, or even sporting events like the Olympics, triathlons, football games, etc.

- **Internal Demand** generators: weddings, celebrations,

congresses, conventions, that are held in your hotel.

- **Circumstantial demand** generators: from the current economic situation to the economic slump or rebounds of other destinations, which may be, for example, a political instability, terrorist attack, etc.

According to how these demand generators affect your hotel or the destination, your occupancy and average price will fluctuate from one year to other in different dates.

What should be also reflected in this calendar are the offers and discounts that can be applied to our customers, such as advanced booking rates or non-refundable rates and we will have to update this calendar every time we change the price of a particular day. This update is going to be very useful because if there is a problem in our PMS or booking program, or if our computer breaks down, we would not know the rates that we were going to use to sell a room on a particular day. If we have the calendar printed out and updated in case of loss of that information we will easily be able to find it. This calendar will also help us to see how often or to which price we have been changing those rates: higher, lower, etc. - it will be helpful in the future to see how much we were selling for on a specific date.

Example of rate calendar:

CALENDAR 2017

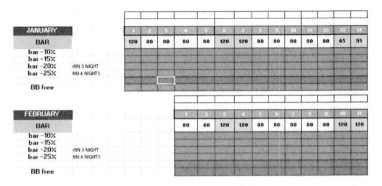

JANUARY

BAR	1	2	3	4	5	6	7	8	9	10	11	12	13	14
	120	80	80	80	80	120	120	80	80	80	80	80	65	95

bar -10%
bar -15%
bar -20% MIN 3 NIGHT
bar -25% MIN 4 NIGHTS

BB free

FEBRUARY

BAR	1	2	3	4	5	6	7	8	9	10	11
	80	80	120	120	80	80	80	80	120	120	

bar -10%
bar -15%
bar -20% MIN 3 NIGHT
bar -25% MIN 4 NIGHTS

BB free

13. THE DEMAND CALENDAR

Having a stable demand eliminates the need for a Revenue Manager. However, tourism demand is often volatile, uncertain and subject to seasonal variations depending on the product of the hotel and its location. Variations in tourism demand force hoteliers to look for different instruments to manage demand – attract more customers during slow periods, attract higher paying customers and divert demand from busy to less busy periods

The demand calendar will allow us to understand what the characteristics of the bookings and of our customers are and it will give us hints to detect the changes that we are getting in our booking system, such as our average daily price, the RevPAR and the occupation. The calendar of demand allows us to look ahead, to forecast the demand and the occupation. It allows us to easily see on what days the bookings are being consolidated, at what rates they are being sold, the volume of bookings and the daily pick up. It allows us to make a comparison with the previous year. Making a demand calendar and checking it daily is very important; it will not only tell us what the situation of our business is today, but what the future looks like.

10%	3	TARIFAS				
Nuestro Hotel	Travelclick	Hotel A	Hotel B	Hotel C	Hotel D	Hotel E
215,0 €	195,45 €	206,36 €	233,75 €	200,00 €	259,00 €	180,91 €
215,0 €	195,45 €	260,91 €	254,15 €	200,00 €	259,00 €	180,91 €
235,0 €	213,64 €	CLOSED	297,50 €	200,00 €	299,00 €	162,73 €
235,0 €	213,64 €	CLOSED	297,50 €	290,00 €	CLOSED	162,73 €
175,0 €	159,09 €	206,36 €	191,25 €	220,00 €	264,00 €	162,73 €
165,0 €	168,18 €	235,18 €	191,25 €	220,00 €	319,00 €	162,73 €
185,0 €	186,36 €	235,18 €	191,25 €	220,00 €	279,00 €	180,91 €
185,0 €	186,36 €	197,27 €	191,25 €	220,00 €	249,00 €	180,91 €
185,0 €	186,36 €	289,45 €	212,50 €	220,00 €	249,00 €	180,91 €
199,0 €	199,09 €	235,18 €	212,50 €	220,00 €	284,00 €	180,91 €
199,0 €	199,09 €	235,18 €	246,50 €	220,00 €	219,00 €	162,73 €
165,0 €	168,18 €	179,09 €	182,75 €	220,00 €	239,00 €	162,73 €
165,0 €	168,18 €	179,09 €	191,25 €	220,00 €	239,00 €	162,73 €
185,0 €	186,36 €	179,09 €	191,25 €	200,00 €	249,00 €	162,73 €
185,0 €	186,36 €	179,09 €	191,25 €	200,00 €	249,00 €	153,64 €
185,0 €	186,36 €	179,09 €	212,50 €	200,00 €	249,00 €	153,64 €
165,0 €	168,18 €	188,18 €	212,50 €	200,00 €	229,00 €	153,64 €
165,0 €	168,18 €	188,18 €	246,50 €	200,00 €	219,00 €	153,64 €
165,0 €	168,18 €	170,00 €	182,75 €	190,00 €	229,00 €	153,64 €
175,0 €	177,27 €	170,00 €	191,25 €	190,00 €	229,00 €	153,64 €
175,0 €	177,27 €	170,00 €	191,25 €	190,00 €	239,00 €	153,64 €
175,0 €	177,27 €	170,00 €	169,15 €	190,00 €	239,00 €	153,64 €
175,0 €	177,27 €	170,00 €	191,25 €	190,00 €	239,00 €	153,64 €
175,0 €	177,27 €	170,00 €	191,25 €	190,00 €	229,00 €	153,64 €

	PICK UP			
E	DB4	AYER	HOY	PROMEDIO
	2	1	4	2
	3	2	3	3
	2	2	2	2
	2	1	2	2
7	3	4	5	4
	2	2	3	2
	2	2	3	2
	3	1	4	3
	2	4	3	3
	0	1	1	1
	0	1	0	0
	1	0	2	1
	4	2	5	4
	1	0	3	1
	1	1	4	2
	2	1	2	2

TARIFAS AYER				
Hotel A	Hotel B	Hotel C	Hotel D	Hotel E
206 €	234 €	200 €	259 €	181 €
261 €	254 €	200 €	259 €	181 €
CLOSED	298 €	200 €	464 €	163 €
CLOSED	298 €	290 €	CLOSED	163 €
206 €	191 €	220 €	264 €	175 €
235 €	191 €	220 €	319 €	163 €
235 €	191 €	220 €	279 €	181 €
197 €	191 €	220 €	249 €	181 €
235 €	213 €	220 €	249 €	181 €
235 €	213 €	220 €	229 €	181 €
235 €	247 €	220 €	219 €	163 €
179 €	183 €	220 €	239 €	163 €

Example of a demand calendar

Tabla de tarifas (documento rotado 90°):

10%	3	TARIFAS					CAMBIOS					PICK UP				TARIFAS AYER				
Nuestro Precio		Hotel A	Hotel B	Hotel C	Hotel D	Hotel E	Hotel A	Hotel B	Hotel C	Hotel D	Hotel E	OBS	AYER	HOY		Hotel A	Hotel B	Hotel C	Hotel D	Hotel E
215,0 €	195,45 €	206,36 €	233,75 €	200,00 €	259,00 €	160,91 €	0,00	0,00	0,00	0,00	0,00	3	1	4	2	206 €	234 €	200 €	259 €	181 €
215,0 €	195,45 €	260,91 €	254,15 €	200,00 €	259,00 €	160,91 €	0,00	0,00	0,00	0,00	0,00	3	2	3	3	261 €	254 €	200 €	259 €	181 €
235,0 €	213,64 €	CLOSED	297,50 €	200,00 €	299,00 €	162,73 €	CERRADO?	0,00	0,00	-165,00	0,00	2	2	2	2	CLOSED	208 €	200 €	464 €	163 €
235,0 €	213,64 €	CLOSED	297,50 €	290,00 €	CLOSED	162,73 €	CERRADO?	0,00	0,00	CERRADO?	0,00	2	1	2	2	CLOSED	208 €	290 €	CLOSED	163 €
173,0 €	159,09 €	206,36 €	191,25 €	220,00 €	264,00 €	162,73 €	0,00	0,00	0,00	0,00	-12,27	3	4	5	4	206 €	191 €	220 €	264 €	175 €
165,0 €	166,18 €	235,18 €	191,25 €	220,00 €	319,00 €	162,73 €	0,00	0,00	0,00	0,00	0,00	2	2	3	2	235 €	191 €	220 €	319 €	163 €
185,0 €	186,36 €	235,18 €	191,25 €	220,00 €	279,00 €	180,91 €	0,00	0,00	0,00	0,00	0,00	2	2	3	2	235 €	191 €	220 €	279 €	181 €
185,0 €	186,36 €	197,27 €	191,25 €	220,00 €	249,00 €	180,91 €	0,00	0,00	0,00	0,00	0,00	3	1	4	3	197 €	191 €	220 €	249 €	181 €
191,0 €	186,36 €	289,45 €	212,50 €	220,00 €	249,00 €	180,91 €	54,27	0,00	0,00	0,00	0,00	2	4	3	3	235 €	213 €	220 €	249 €	181 €
199,0 €	199,09 €	235,18 €	212,50 €	220,00 €	286,00 €	180,91 €	0,00	0,00	0,00	55,00	0,00	0	1	1	1	235 €	238 €	220 €	229 €	181 €
199,0 €	199,09 €	235,18 €	246,50 €	220,00 €	219,00 €	162,73 €	0,00	0,00	0,00	0,00	0,00	0	1	0	1	235 €	247 €	220 €	219 €	163 €
165,0 €	168,18 €	179,09 €	182,75 €	220,00 €	239,00 €	162,73 €	0,00	0,00	0,00	0,00	0,00	1	2	2	0	179 €	183 €	220 €	239 €	163 €
185,0 €	168,18 €	168,18 €	191,25 €	220,00 €	239,00 €	162,73 €	0,00	0,00	0,00	0,00	0,00	4	2	3	4	179 €	191 €	220 €	239 €	163 €
185,0 €	186,36 €	179,09 €	191,25 €	200,00 €	249,00 €	153,64 €	0,00	0,00	0,00	0,00	0,00	1	0	1	1	179 €	191 €	200 €	249 €	154 €
185,0 €	186,36 €	179,09 €	191,25 €	200,00 €	249,00 €	153,64 €	0,00	0,00	0,00	0,00	0,00	1	1	2	1	179 €	191 €	200 €	249 €	154 €
165,0 €	158,18 €	188,18 €	212,50 €	200,00 €	229,00 €	153,64 €	0,00	0,00	0,00	0,00	0,00	1	1	1	1	188 €	213 €	200 €	229 €	154 €
165,0 €	164,18 €	188,18 €	246,50 €	200,00 €	229,00 €	153,64 €	0,00	0,00	0,00	0,00	3,64	1	1	0	1	188 €	247 €	200 €	229 €	150 €
165,0 €	164,16 €	170,00 €	182,75 €	190,00 €	229,00 €	153,64 €	0,00	0,00	0,00	0,00	0,00	2	3	1	1	170 €	183 €	190 €	229 €	154 €
175,0 €	177,27 €	170,80 €	191,25 €	190,00 €	239,00 €	153,64 €	0,00	0,00	0,00	0,00	0,00	2	3	3	3	170 €	191 €	190 €	239 €	154 €
175,0 €	177,27 €	170,00 €	191,25 €	190,00 €	239,00 €	153,64 €	0,00	0,00	0,00	0,00	0,00	2	4	4	2	170 €	169 €	190 €	239 €	154 €
175,0 €	177,27 €	170,00 €	169,15 €	190,00 €	239,00 €	153,64 €	0,00	0,00	0,00	0,00	0,00	2	0	1	1	170 €	191 €	190 €	239 €	154 €
175,0 €	177,27 €	170,00 €	191,25 €	190,00 €	239,00 €	153,64 €	0,00	0,00	0,00	0,00	0,00	1	0	0	1	170 €	191 €	190 €	239 €	154 €
175,0 €	177,27 €	170,00 €	233,75 €	190,00 €	219,00 €	153,64 €	0,00	0,00	0,00	0,00	0,00	1	1	0	1	170 €	234 €	190 €	219 €	154 €
165,0 €	158,18 €	170,00 €	182,75 €	190,00 €	209,00 €	153,64 €	0,00	0,00	0,00	-28,00	0,00	1	0	2	1	170 €	163 €	190 €	264 €	154 €
155,0 €	158,18 €	170,00 €	191,25 €	190,00 €	239,00 €	153,64 €	0,00	0,00	0,00	0,00	0,00	1	1	1	1	170 €	191 €	190 €	239 €	154 €
175,0 €	177,27 €	170,00 €	191,25 €	190,00 €	239,00 €	153,64 €	0,00	0,00	0,00	-19,68	0,00	1	1	1	1	170 €	191 €	190 €	239 €	154 €
175,0 €	177,27 €	170,00 €	191,25 €	190,00 €	254,00 €	153,64 €	0,00	0,00	0,00	0,00	0,00	1	0	1	1	170 €	191 €	190 €	274 €	154 €
165,0 €	168,18 €	170,00 €	191,25 €	190,00 €	229,00 €	153,64 €	0,00	0,00	0,00	0,00	0,00	1	2	1	1	170 €	191 €	190 €	229 €	154 €
165,0 €	168,18 €	170,00 €	212,50 €	190,00 €	219,00 €	153,64 €	0,00	0,00	0,00	0,00	0,00	1	0	0	0	170 €	213 €	190 €	229 €	154 €

14. FORECASTING

Another very important tool that we have to prepare weekly is the **Forecasting**. The Forecasting is the management of the future demand - what we think, predict or deduct that we will generate in room revenue and occupation. It is important to have a weekly meeting with the General Manager and the sales team to make them familiar with the booking tendencies of our property in the current month and the following 2 months. The Forecast gives you a picture of how the business is doing and how will it be performing in the forthcoming days and months. It consists of making an estimation of the demand by analyzing historical data and the predictions and tendencies that we have. It allows us to compare the previous years and detect which segments are evolving favorably and which not and allows us to adjust the sales strategy on a timely basis. For example, if in a particular month we estimated that we would have many reservations from the leisure segment and these bookings are not coming in, we should have the capacity and time to react and check both our prices and the competitor's prices, make promotions and make new contracts with other distributors, etc.

It is very important to prepare this document (the Forecasting) so that we get a picture of how our business is doing. It is important to have all the information related to the different segments of our property in this spreadsheet so that we can analyze their evolution.

To make a good analysis we must take into account the socioeconomic times (wars, crises, etc.) in which we are or have been operating and identify and consider if there has been or there is a change in shopping habits (for example, if customers are booking less days, more in advance, if they book packages, with tour operators, from a particular geographic region etc.). Today in Europe the market has evolved with more bookings at the last minute, and this is because clients have changed their buying habits from previously, when they would be buying package holidays in advance. Nowadays, people have access to internet services and products and anyone can make bookings from their mobile phone or laptop with a very short check-in time. And it happens the same with plane tickets, trains, car rentals, etc. The customer can book all of these services by himself, without a third person or a travel agency in the middle, so the time invested to purchase is lower.

In order to make a forecast as realistic as possible we have to consider group reservations, pick up results and the booking curve.

GROUP RESERVATIONS

A follow up of the group bookings will have to be conducted correctly and you will have to write down, in an Excel document, all of the requests received each month, the price and the conversion of those bookings. This will be useful to establish the group's strategy and its prices (the dates on which you would want to offer lower prices, higher prices and how long the minimum number of nights stay should be etc.)

What do we have to consider when receiving group bookings?

- the conversion ratio

- anticipation and cancellation ratios

- amount spent per group

- the size of a group (number of rooms booked and occupation rates)

- the segment each group belongs to (leisure, business, congresses, FIT etc.)

BOOKING CURVE

Building a booking curve will help you to visualize how the pick up and reservations are evolving, in particular those clients who have confirmed and those who have cancelled their bookings. You will be able to identify if your prices are affecting your sales and to forecast future bookings.

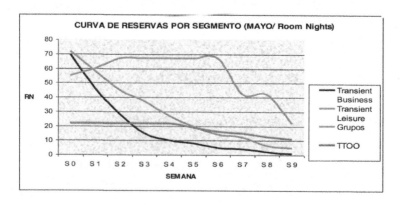

PICK UP

The pick up helps us to see how bookings are evolving. You can calculate a daily, weekly or monthly pick up figure.

In order to make a control we have, for instance, the confirmed bookings that we have on the 1st of January for all that month of the year. The following week we will check how many bookings we have and we will see how the sales are doing.

Month	OTB (1th Jan)	OTB (8 th Jan)	DIF
January	350	385	35
February	150	195	45

CONTROL OF THE STAY

One of the biggest headaches of Revenue and Sales departments is over-demand and overselling on specific dates. For example, imagine that on 2nd March your hotel has 35 spare rooms still to be sold, on the 3rd March your hotel is fully booked and on the 4th March there are still 40 rooms that have not been booked.

What exactly has happened and what could you have possibly done in order to increase the chance that all those rooms would have been booked on the day immediately before and after the 3rd March? Well, if a detailed follow-up of demand and bookings had been conducted correctly, we would have detected that on 3rd March the hotel would have been full and that we should have controlled/altered both the length of the minimum stays and also the first reservation date that would have been available to be booked. In this particular case, a possible option would have been to create either a 2 or 3 night minimum length of stay condition and to have made either 2nd or 3rd March the only permitted days of arrival, we would also have to refuse all the bookings for 1 night only (from the 2nd March to 4th March). This approach could potentially increase the number of bookings on the days immediately before and/or after 3rd March.

15. BENCHMARKING

Benchmarking is the comparison of our business, the hotel, restaurant or bar, against other competitors. To do this, we will first of all need to determine who are our competitors. A competitor cannot be another business that offers a service that doesn't resemble at all what we offer in our business. We may consider that they are our competitors by quarter, by region, by category. We will need to determine what sets us apart from them, and what makes us different.

Benchmarking will allow us to develop extensive knowledge not only of rates, but also of the added value that we can offer.

The benchmarking of our competitors will include looking at their:

- prices

- the locations

- the services they offer

- their product

- their distribution channels

We will have to study the competition in order to know what prices consumers in each segment are typically booking rooms for, so that we can anticipate our rivals' strategies and how to respond to them.

If we have a 60-room boutique hotel and most of our sales are made through OTAs but 10% is sold through TTOO or bed banks our pricing strategy will be different from that of a hotel that has 300 rooms and that needs to fill those 300 rooms every day, since it will surely have group series agreements and corporate rates that are lower to those offered online. We will have to ask to ourselves how the strategies of our rivals would affect the demand levels of our hotel?

EVALUATE THE SOURCES OF ADDED VALUE OF YOUR COMPETITORS

strengths + weaknesses = value

To analyze the value that a hotel can offer we will consider:

- who our competitors are

- make a check list of our products and assess how they compare to those of our competitors, which will include looking at variables such as: location, customer service, cleanliness, number of restaurants and bars, swimming pools, meeting rooms, the efficiency of the booking process, in-room amenities, decorations, etc.

- identify the weaknesses and strengths of our hotel and

rate them on the same check list.

With these data sources we will be able to obtain a score that shows us how we compare (rank) to rival hotels. This will undoubtedly be a factor that will influence the hotel's pricing policy and what we can expect from the demand in result of the quality / price ratio comparison with our competitors.

You can also quickly check how customers evaluate your hotel and your competitors on various measures by looking at ratings on Booking.com or on Expedia pages, an example of such data being shown below:

Do a monthly comparison, to check how the performance of your hotel is doing, either going up or down.

We can then ask ourselves whether we are attracting the clients that we would expect that would correspond to our offer of quality and product service and also whether we are realistically in position to get clients that may pay more for a room and other services of our hotel.

Take some time to analyze your competitors regularly, so that you can see how you can improve in relation to them. For instance, you can: change the decorations of the rooms, replace the shower curtains, build a swimming pool if viable or offer a pick-up and drop-off service from and to the airport, etc. All those sources of added value can at a relatively low cost lead you customers who prefer you over the competition (especially nowadays, when the information that the hotels are offering is easily reachable online).

Tools for the benchmarking analysis

There's a series of tools that help us to study benchmarking, such as **Star Global**. Star Global is a company dedicated to sending daily data comparisons of our business with our competitors, which will have previously designated.

Daily, we are going to fill the average price we had the day before and what was our occupation; they will send us a few different reports, one that will inform us about our average price, our RevPAR and our occupation, in comparison with the competition. They will also send us weekly reports with the week's data, and the monthly one with the data of the last thirty days. We will be able to compare how are we performing and how our competitors are doing; it will be useful to establish pricing strategies, and to improve our services or what we are offering. It is a good tool to know and see how our strategy is evolving.

	E	F	G	H	I	J	K	L	M	N	O	P	Q	R	S	T	U	V	W	X	Y	Z	AA	AB	AC
20	36.7	-26.3		38.4	3.0		33.3	-15.7		29.5	-29.8		42.2	19.5		77.0	40.6		89.7	9.2		44.9	-6.1		

Running 28 Days (by Day of Week)

Sunday	% Chg	Monday	% Chg	Tuesday	% Chg	Wednesday	% Chg	Thursday	% Chg	Friday	% Chg	Saturday	% Chg	Total	% Chg
51.1%	6.5	44.3%	3.3	40.1%	-16.6	43.2%	-0.7	44.9%	-7.1	49.7%	-10.3	63.9%	7.1	48.2%	-2.3
49.1%	6.3	49.7%	4.6	55.6%	0.8	64.3%	17.3	57.9%	18.5	56.7%	16.3	66.0%	17.2	55.5%	11.4
104.2	0.2	89.2	-1.1	72.0	-16.2	67.1	-15.3	77.6	-21.6	87.7	-22.2	116.2	-8.6	86.9	-12.3
57.36	-2.7	67.24	-19.5	70.60	-30.5	83.06	126.1	37.52	-0.9	52.47	24.2	61.64	8.7	59.07	2.8
72.24	1.6	73.75	-10.6	81.84	-3.4	90.68	22.1	79.28	12.4	61.88	-8.9	68.98	-0.3	75.92	1.9
79.4	-4.3	91.2	-10.0	86.1	-28.1	91.6	86.1	47.3	-11.9	84.8	36.2	75.0	9.1	77.8	0.9
29.33	3.6	29.80	-16.9	28.24	-41.3	35.88	124.6	16.84	-7.9	26.09	11.4	33.01	16.5	28.46	0.4
36.45	8.0	36.62	-4.6	46.52	-2.6	58.34	43.3	45.87	33.2	35.09	5.1	37.88	16.8	42.11	13.6
82.7	-4.1	81.4	-11.0	62.0	-39.7	61.5	56.7	36.7	-30.9	74.3	6.0	87.1	-0.3	67.6	-11.5

Table of Contents | Glance | Daily by Month | Daily by Month Ind | Occ | ADR | RevPAR | Response | Help

In this chart we can see, for example, the occupation graph, the average price and the RevPAR index.

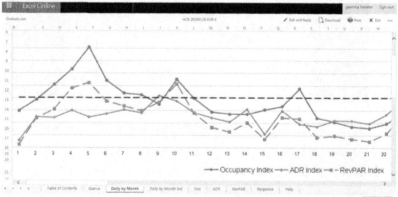

—•— Occupancy Index —•— ADR Index —■— RevPAR Index

Another tool of Benchmarking is **Price Match.**

Price Match is a very easy tool to use and is very visual. According to the company, it allows us to increase our RevPAR, which is basically useful to see the evolution of the occupation that we had in the past, what we have now and where it is heading to.

It shows us to what price we have changed the room prices and it recommends an optimal price to us that, according to this evolution, would be the ideal one to sell those last rooms. It's a quite useful tool to prepare the forecast and, with other reports and statistics, it can help us to decide at what price we should be selling our rooms.

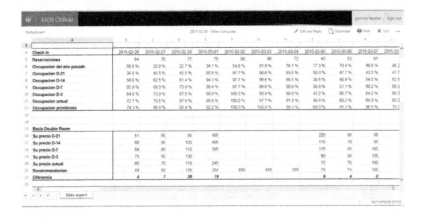

Other tools that we can use are those that tell us our about competitor's prices within a period of up to a year. It's really useful because it saves us a lot of time as we can get those reports daily directly in our email or even several times per day - and we don't have to manually check the prices.

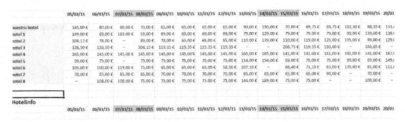

16. PRICING

Pricing is the optimization of sales through a pricing strategy. Pricing can also be external; it has to do with the competition and positioning, both our own and that of our competitors.

Pricing is the placement and mental perception of a customer or consumer of our brand, in this case our hotel, and of what differentiates us from our competitors. The placement of our product and of our hotel has to match the pricing policy; that means that, for example, our perception normally associates a brand or luxury products with high prices. In our mind a luxury hotel or five stars is associated with good service, good rooms, good quality of sleep, with friendly and helpful employees, with an X quality food at breakfast ... and all this also coincides with a high price. In the mind of a customer, they will never think that a 4 or 5 star hotel is going to cost the same as a hostel and so they will not expect the same services; for this reason we cannot sell a hostel room at the same price as a 5 star hotel - we have to position and sell our product by associating it with a good pricing policy, selling it at the right price.

Until 2006, most hotels operated with static rates, that is, a fixed price for weekdays and a different price for weekends; or one general price for the Winter season and one general price for the Summer season. However, since 2006 the BAR (best available rate) approach become widespread and since then most hotels have been working with variable rates across different prices ranges according to different levels of supply and demand on specific days of the week, month, season or year.

A fixed rate approach, while more simple to apply, can however lead to a loss of revenue or profit and so it is advisable to offer more than one price and more than one type of product in order to maximise sales and the range of customers that you can attract. This in economics, is known as, price discrimination.

Why should a hotel offer different types of rooms at different prices? For example, a family that needs more space in a room will be willing to pay € 40 more for having a larger room.

Or a couple who wants a romantic stay may well be willing to pay for a premium room and services that gives them access to a hotel's spa or romantic dinner while perhaps a businessman/businesswoman may not want to use such facilities and may simply want a room and breakfast only, which would imply that they would be willing/looking to pay a different rate.

You can offer as many prices and packages as you want. You must consider how you can design and combine the 4Ps in the Marketing Mix (here we are focusing on price and product in particular rather than place and promotion) to maximise your sales, revenues and profit.

A CALL TO ACTION

- Evaluate what products your customers would be willing to buy or what they buy from your competitors.

- Make a list of the types of rooms you could offer and the special services you could add (for example: standard rooms, superior rooms, spa passes, rooms with breakfast and parking spaces etc.)

- Decide what supplementary prices could be set for the add-ons that you can offer.

- Differentiate the products that you sell in each distribution channel.

A product is the combination of its price and its value. There are different types of clients with different needs, so we must anticipate who they are and what they want and offer them what we think they may want or need.

Try to prepare a grill with different ranges of bar rates with different restrictions (minimum nights, non-refundable rate, etc.) and a month later see how your sales have gone and your reservation anticipation.

The logical thing to do would seem to be to set a "cheaper pricing" strategy for clients that make early reservations and increase rates as soon as availability falls for a particular date and increase rates for a check in dates as those dates get closer to the current date. However, in many cases this theory is not the best one to follow in practice and what may happen is that if we set a certain rate but rooms do not sell, we in practice end up lowering prices as the relevant check in date approached. This second approach is called price cannibalism and many customers have become aware of this being a common practice in our sector so they have started to wait for last-minute deals.

PRICE PARITY

The goal of any hotel should be to have price parity for all online sales. What this means is having the same price being offered for the same room/service on different websites and hotels want to achieve this so that customers end up buying from the website that suits the hotel the most.

As a hotel, we will be more interested in selling through our own page since we will save commissions charged by third party websites, which can be up to 30%.

It will be more profitable to sell a room on your own website, which may generate a 1.5% commission in comparison to Booking.com, which charges around 18% in commissions.

A €100 booking with 1.5% commission = € 98.50 income

A €100 with 18% commissionS = € 82 income

Currently, many hotels are choosing to offer their clients cheaper rates through their own website with a discount for non-refundable bookings or for bookings that have cancellation periods that end far in advance of the dates of the actual booking. This can encourage customers to book through their own site rather than through OTAs and in this way, despite offering a discount of around 10 to 15% for such bookings made through their own sites, a hotel can manage to make a greater profit than if it completed that sale through an OTA.

17. CREATE VALUE, INCREASE REVENUE

Value is much discussed in the academic field and considered a marketing concept. Neap & Celik (1999) state that the 'value of a product reflects the owner(s)'/buyer(s)' desire to retain or obtain a product'.

For this reason, following their definition, the product has value for both the hotel and its guests. Value is defined

- ✓ *in the economic way* as: The worth of all the benefits and rights arising from ownership. Two types of economic value are (1) the utility of a good or service, and (2) power of a good or service to command other goods, services, or money, in voluntary exchange.
- ✓ And in a *marketing way* it is defined as: The extent to which a good or service is perceived by its customer to meet his or her needs or wants, measured by customer's willingness to pay for it. It commonly depends more on the customer's

perception of the worth of the product than on its intrinsic value.

The *expected value* is what the customer thinks that he can get from a product or a service during or after its consumption can be expected, while the perceived value is the actual value obtained by a customer.

The product or services that a hotel provides can be perceived as tangible or intangible: (Stanislav Ivanov (2014). *Hotel Revenue Management: From Theory to Practice)*

  ✓ *Tangible hotel product attributes* – location, hotel facilities, room amenities, room view, design of the hotel, colours, odour, space utilisation, wifi, services, etc.
  ✓ *Intangible hotel product attributes* – servicemindedness of the personnel (helpfulness, responsiveness, friendliness, courtesy), speed of the service, service personalisation, safety, atmosphere, etc.

Tangible attributes are easy to copy by competitors but the intangible are not. And those are the ones in which your property should be focused. It will get your customers attention and probably it will be very appreciated. It will be at this point, when your property will be able to increase prices and set them higher than your competitors.

18. MANAGING THE SALES CHANNELS

What does a Revenue Manager have to do as part of his/her job? He/she has to manage multiple sales channels. And they are:

- **The website of the hotel.** Needless to say, a hotel or a property should have its own website to sell as much as is possible through its own booking system. Depending on what type of booking system your property has, the commission you pay is zero or it will be much lower than the one charged by the OTA's; for this reason it's our objective to sell as many rooms as possible through our own website. In order to have a good volume of reservations through it, this website has to be well developed, functional, intuitive and easy to use, so that our customers can book in a few clicks.

- The **OTA's**. The Online Travel Agencies are those agencies that, as the word says, work online. Some of them are, for example, Booking.com, Expedia, Lastminute, Easytobook, etc. Currently, this is where most of the bookings of most of the properties come from. These websites show the availability of the hotel in real time, the different prices and room categories, and they have pictures of the property and its services, with a complete description.

The rates have to be the same on all of the OTA's. There's a big "war" with the disparities (different prices offered by different OTA's) in order to get customers. Some of them reduce their commissions in order to sell a room at a price of €93, for instance, instead of €95.

- The **IDS** are booking systems through which many companies and many agencies make reservations.

- **Tour Operators** (Tour Operation) are the wholesalers who act as intermediaries between agencies and clients. Usually the properties sign a 6-month contract or a 1-year contract with established rates and a certain availability. Usually rates cannot increase but can decrease if you realize that you gave a too-high price to a tour operator because you were expecting to sell at a higher rate in a particular period.

These are the different channels through which a hotel usually sells its rooms, but there might be other contracts signed with traditional travel agencies or companies with which a property might have a compromised allotment and rates.

19. THE CHANNEL MANAGER

Most of the properties and hotels have software that allows them to introduce the bookings, set the prices and manage the billing of its customers. An example of this software would be Opera, Tesipro or any other that allows you to manage reservations, make statistics, analyze data, and set the room rates.

This software is usually connected to a Channel Manager. The Channel Manager is software that is used to avoid having to manually change the prices on the different websites with which the hotels have a distribution contract (Booking.com, Expedia, Easytobook etc.), as it could be really long and ardous work having to manually change the rates of all the rooms and all the days in all the channels. Due to the volume of contracted channels (in some hotels the amount of contracts could be fifteen or twenty websites) the use of Channel Manager is more than welcome.

Some of the most commonly used are Rate Tiger and SiteMinder.

These portals allow us to manage and send information about our availability changes, rates, and closing and opening sales to various channels with which we have a signed contract with and in which we are selling our rooms.

This tool has also other functions, such as revenue analysis per channel; it also allows you to see the reservations and cancellations, and if you have connectivity issues with a particular channel. What it basically does is make the work of the Revenue Manager a little bit easier, so that they can spend more time on developing a pricing strategy and sales, and less on the manual labor required to change rates on all portals with which we have signed a contract.

To summarize the functions of the Channel Manager:

- We have all the Ota's on a single platform

- We can see availability and rates

- It keeps the pricing strategy and availability, avoiding manual errors

- We can control availability

- We can better control the bookings and cancellations

- We can get statistics: average stay per site, revenue, etc.

This tool obviously has a cost but it's very useful, so I would recommend it to any professional to use it as it will save you a lot of time.

20. DUMPING

Dumping is the practice of some online agencies to lower prices to benefit from the sales produced in the channel due to this price difference.

Dumping is also the resale of "beds" between distributors. The fact is that OTA's ask for parity of prices so that all of them have the same prices and the same opportunity to sell a room. When some online agencies or distributors resell the "beds" of a hotel, sometimes they do not respect this price parity and sell those beds at a lower price.

To fight against dumping, some tools have been created to make all of this fight and work more bearable by allowing control from a single page to discover if there are any price differences across the various sites.

Usually, most of the online agencies have this tool and tend to send price disparities to the hotels if they find out that its competitor is selling a room at a lower price.

In order to check which distributor is causing dumping to our property there are **two** ways that will help us in this work.

1. If we find a site that is offering a lower rate than the one it should be, we should make a booking to our own property; when we choose the method of payment: cash on arrival or transfer, upon receiving the voucher, we can see who has resold the room to this agency.

2. Another way to try to find out is to see if there's any name of the original provider on the website of the vendor.

SECTION 3. MARKETING YOUR BUSINESS

21. ONLINE MARKETING

In order to sell our hotel as best as we can, we count with the same tools that any other company may choose with regard to online marketing.

Online Marketing allows us to take advantage of our online presence using the different online platforms in order to try to sell our product and our brand to our potential customers.

Online Marketing allow us to seize internet platforms with online presence to try to sell our product, our brand to our potential clients.

In the case before us, that is the case of the hotels, we can carry out a variety of marketing campaigns:

- email marketing

- google AdWords

- managing online reputation (answering the comments people leave us)

- our brand needs to be present in social media (blog, Facebook, Instagram, twitter...)

- invest in meta-search engines of our own web page

Let's assess each one of these tools in order to sell our accommodation and increase our revenue. Because the correct management of our social media and our online reputation may directly influence our average price and occupancy!

How do our clients find the hotel?

There are different ways for a client to find our hotel and decide to book a room with us, rather than with the competition.

One way is to **make a booking through an online agency or TTOO**. In that case, we cannot control much as it will depend on the characteristics of the hotel that the client is looking for (pool, gym, 3 stars, downtown...), the rating and the price. But we can control the price and rating, which will be a reflection of the perception of the price-quality ratio, and the assessment of the hotel services. A hotel with good assessment may be between the highest positions and the first pages of the different agencies and, clearly, a hotel with the same facilities/characteristics and price, but a better rating than the competition, will receive more bookings. This is why the online rating affects the revenue and the sales of an accommodation.

A second way of doing online marketing is starting an

email marketing campaign, which would promote the hotel through its newsletter. In order to do that, it is very important to collect the client's emails at the moment of the check-in. Once we have them, we can send promotions and discounts directly to their emails, so that the next time that they book our hotel, they will do it directly with us and we will save the commission of those 3rd party travel agencies.

The third way is having an **online presence on social media** through our official accounts: twitter, Instagram, Facebook... we will need someone to be directly responsible for its management, and it has to be directed with formal language, with standards that every social media understands, we will also need to create a well-planned strategy for social media. We must consider that practically most of the population has a smart phone with internet access, and most of the people have an account on those social networks. It is not surprising that a future client will visit our official profiles to obtain information of the hotel (see photographs, ask for information, check the location, check how the complaints and recommendation were managed, etc.)

The fourth way to find us online is doing an accommodation research on an **online search engine** (For example Google) and search for a hotel in Miami or a specific hotel by its name.

To do this there are different types of results on those searches:

- paid search (ads= AdWords)

- organic search

In this example we can see the paid advertisement by the hotel in the top position; this is to capture leads, and the second result shows the organic one, this is the one that the hotel is not paying. Some years ago a new law stated that websites of brands (hotels) must be able to appear before Booking or Expedia websites.

There are several types of advertisements:

- network research (the above ad)

- display network (those that pop up with photos on the pages such as The New York times, or any website)

- Network search with display selection

- shopping

- Video

- and universal campaign of applications.

To do these kinds of paid advertisement we will need to create a Google AdWords account so we can plan our ad campaign with the most accurate keywords at a cost per bid.

The keywords are the words the tourist will enter in the search engines to find the hotel he/she is looking for.

When someone is searching for a hotel, usually these are the terms that are used:

- *Hotels*

- *Hotels + geographical criterion* (for example: Hotels in

Madrid)

- Hotels + geographical criterion + amenities (for example: Hotels in Madrid with spa)

The problem is that each word has a cost and we will not be able to compete with our competition, so it is important to follow a series of recommendations that allow us to adjust the words that our clients are going to type to reach our target audience.

What should I consider when choosing the keywords?

As we have said before, keywords have to be a reflection of the inquiries your potential customers may have.

It is critical to consider how people search for our hotel but, above all, it is crucial to remove words that do not generate visits.

The process to select the key words has to be based on:

- The **hotel web page**: it is crucial to choose the keywords that are related with your web content. For example, if we put a hotel in Madrid with a spa, it must have a spa, or a budget hotel in Madrid, it must not be an expensive hotel, etc.

- The **products** and **amenities** provided: What are the ones that makes us different from the competition? ex. *hotels for adults in Miami; hotels with fitness center in Barcelona.*

- and combine **our brand with our products or amenities**; *ex. hotels near the Sagrada Família, hotels near Palma de Mallorca beaches.*

The bids. AdWords auctions

<u>CPC or Cost per click</u>

How can I win the bid against my competitors?

First of all, Google will take into account the maximum price you are willing to pay per click, although you will never get to pay that price since Google will consider the reference value that your competitor will had previously set.

Secondly, Google will take into account the following variables in order to measure the quality of the ad:

1. The quality of the destination page

2. The importance of the keywords

3. The percentage of clicks

The result of multiplying the maximum bid price by the quality of the ad will determine your position in the search engine.

And, how does Google establish the cost by click? The search engine divides the obtained result of multiplying the maximum bid price by the level of quality of the ad, of my immediately previous competitor and by the score obtained in my quality level.

For example:

Think about 3 different hotels: A, B and C. Hotel A has a maximum of € 4 per bid, B € 3 and C € 2.

And Google has stated that in terms of quality hotel A has a 5, B has 9 and C has 7.

The ranking is:

Hotel A= 4 x 5 = 20 (2º)

Hotel B= 3 x 9= 27 (1º)

Hotel C= 2 x 7= 14 (3º)

The cost value per click would be:

Hotel A= 14/5= 2,8€

Hotel B= 20/9 = 2,22€

Hotel C= minimum price

CPTI or Cost per thousand impressions

The CPTI is used in the display network. The advertiser does not pay per click but for thousand impressions of the ad.

Usually, this type of strategy is used when what you are looking for is to position the position the brand to the detriment of a more aggressive and conversion-oriented sales strategy.

CPA or Cost per Acquisition

The CPA is associated to the conversion rate: It is the cost Google will assign us when a reserve is formalized through our ad.

For example: let's imagine that we are making a campaign with CPA, then the average price of the booking will be of 100€ and the net profit of the hotel is 45€. For the campaign to be profitable, the cost per acquisition must be lower than 45€. If we want to obtain a 30% of benefits on the purchase price, then the CPA should not exceed the 11€.

Now we are going to assess the **metasearch** engines. If we do a specific search for a hotel again, in this case the Gran Havana hotel in Barcelona, we will find the result of the hotel and a search engine for booking dates on the right side on Google.

In this case, we can see that the hotel is paying to appear in the engine for availability, as it will also appear in webs like for example Kayak o Trivago, in order to provide the option for customers to book through their own websites and thus save the commission to third parties. Usually, the hotel will pay the CPC to appear on those search engines.

Gran Hotel Havana

Sitio web   Cómo llegar   Guardar

4,3 ★★★★★ 1.269 reseñas de Google
Hotel de 4 estrellas

RESERVA UNA HABITACIÓN

Dirección: Gran Via de les Corts Catalanes, 647, 08010 Barcelona
Teléfono: 933 41 70 00

Anuncios · Comprobar la disponibilidad

| 📅 dom., 17 may. | 📅 lun., 18 may. | 👥 2 |

Gran Hotel Havana Barcelona Sitio oficial Cancelación Gratuita · Mejor Precio Garantizado	106 € >
Hurb.com	116 € >
Expedia.es	119 € >
FindHotel	109 € >

Mostrar todo   ✕

They can also search through other search engines or specific pages such as TripAdvisor, Facebook or through ads displayed in Google. They can also look for references on different social networking platforms, such as Twitter.

What influences a customer's purchase decision? The information about the hotel, customer comments that can be found on the internet, and of course the price. TripAdvisor is nowadays the most visited website for hotels and restaurants reviews. The founders of TripAdvisor were a married Australian couple who went on holidays and started a website of references and reviews of the places that they visited. This platform hasn't stopped growing since then and now offers direct reservations to restaurants and hotels, and compares hotel prices through various portals by comparing prices of OTA's integrated into their website.

TripAdvisor has both supporters and opponents as it's an open platform where anyone can leave a review and the site does not ask for a previous booking on that property, hotel or restaurant. Some properties have had problems with negative fake reviews left by their competitors in order to try to damage its reputation.

TripAdvisor usually has a department that is responsible for dealing with possible messages and comments that are not true; there has also been the case of hotels, bars and services that have complained that the competition was trying to harm them.

In order to influence the purchase of a possible client, we have to put the same information about our establishment on all channels and be as detailed as possible to encourage our customers to choose us over the competition. That means that if, for example, we have a pool, we have to make that information accessible - so that if a customer is looking for a hotel with a pool in Barcelona, they will be able to find it through our description and will choose us from amongst other competitors.

We also need to include some good and attractive photos. Often there are businesses who forget the effect that a good picture can have; as nowadays we are heading towards a very visual consumption of products and services, we need to offer our product as attractively and with as much detail as possible.

In hotels or bars and restaurants, we can make use of the different platforms of **social media** such as Facebook, which is used by most hotels, Instagram, LinkedIn, YouTube, Tumblr, Pinterest and Twitter. These are the leading platforms and most of the users that use social networks have an account for them. For this reason, we should make an effort to use them and to engage with our potential customers on there. The most used, and with most users, are Facebook, Instagram and Twitter; if you don't have much time available to manage them, you should focus on those ones in order to develop a good social media strategy and dedicate your efforts to these three platforms to create a good base of fans, attract customers and retain them for future stays in your city and in your hotel.

In the next picture we can see examples of hotels that have their establishments with their own website on Facebook and which have X number of likes and visits. These hotels upload photos of events and what is happening in their establishments, and engage with future and past customers and allow them to see that they have an X reputation, and that X people have trusted them.

There have been huge mistakes committed by different establishments and businesses in which social media management has been run in a bad way and this has caused a drop in sales, the loss of the trust of their customers, and damage to its reputation as a company. So it is very important to establish a good social media strategy and to train the people in charge for proper implementation.

Here we can see an example of a well ran communication campaign with a forgotten teddy bear. http://www.mirror.co.uk/news/world-news/lost-toy-bunny-gets-vip-7170138

"LOST TOY BUNNY GETS VIP TREATMENT AFTER LITTLE GIRL LEAVES IT AT HOTEL - BEFORE PAIR ARE REUNITED

The stuffed toy was treated to a life of luxury

when it was forgotten from a family break - and the hotel posted Facebook updates"

Thanks to this, the hotel got a huge promotion for free on the newspapers and online but also its personnel is perceived as caring and friendly.

22. ONLINE REPUTATION

The online reputation is basically what people say about us on the Internet. Why is online reputation and the good management of it important? We will talk more about this topic but online reputation could influence, especially when selling and fixing your prices. Currently, online travel agencies show the ratings of our properties left by our customers based on their experience. What happens for example in Booking.com? The ratings that our guests have given to us will influence our image and reputation and will influence other future customers.

For example, here we can see that the H10 Metropolitan is more valued (with 9.1) than Catalonia Passeig de Gracia (with 9). These are hotels with similar prices, but a customer might decide to book a room in the one with a highest rating and better comments. Ratings consider the service, price, quality, staff and facilities. We must bear in mind that good reputation management is the key to good sales.

There are also some companies that are exclusively dedicated to the management and analysis of the online comments that the customer makes. One of this companies is **Reviewpro**. These tools gather every comment that appear online and give us an average of our establishment, so it will be very useful to see how we can differentiate ourselves and how we can improve.

How to manage online reputation

In order to show to your customers that you consider their opinions and that you really take them seriously, I recommend you manage your online reputation. You should reply to the comments on TripAdvisor and on the online travel agencies where your customers leave reviews.

How to reply to the guests' reviews and comments

Customize your answers

Make every answer unique and original. To do so, use

the customer's name or last name (if you have one). Take time to write a personalized message. Show them how much you care about their valuable comment and about every one of your customers.

Do not only give a 'thanks' as a response to a positive comment. Thank this customer and comment on his/her visit and how happy you are that you have had them in your establishment.

Exclusive answers

Maximize your customer's satisfaction and ensure that each response is unique and specific.

Turn the negative into positive

Although if your client leaves one or several bad reviews about your establishment and services, seek to take this opportunity to report on the planned improvements, those made or what you will have in mind for the future. Be original and look for opportunities to enhance the experience of your customers.

Check out what you've written

It costs nothing to re-read what you've written and make sure you are expressing and writing it correctly.

23. WHAT IS THE SALARY OF A REVENUE MANAGER

Based on a quick study that I have made obtaining data via the internet, as at April 2016 we can say that most of the job advertisements posted online do not show how much salary is offered to a Revenue Manager; for those were the salary was disclosed, the offers were:

In Spain the average salary is €28,000 year / Gross - these positions are in Barcelona, Madrid and Mallorca, in 4*, 5* hotels and management companies or apartments.

In USA, according to payscale.com the average salary is $55,000.

In Australia, the average salary is AUS$65,000

In the UK (in London is where salaries are higher) the average is 45,000 pounds (about €61,000)

And the job descriptions include:

- Analysis and control of the company prices and competition.

- Knowledge of the competitions' activity.
- To ensure the best price and positioning in each segment and season.
- To analyze the behavior of the segments and the demand.
- Identify new opportunities and participate in creating new commercial packages.
- Management of the company's web content with the content manager.
- Work in coordination with the sales department to implement the necessary actions to achieve the objectives.
- Maximize the return on the corporate website of the company and online travel agents.

- Optimization of the presence of the hotel in terms of positioning, content, photos and outstanding presence.

- Price control
- Occupancy control
- Management of the web and content control
- Management of sales closures
- Writing reports and statistics

- Data analysis, occupation results, trends, behaviors and channel productivity and make proposals for improvement.

Incentives and bonuses for goals are also offered.

24. CONCLUSION

And now we have come to the end of this introductory book in Revenue Management in a hotel.

I hope that it has been helpful and that it has served as a good basis to implement strategy in order to get the most benefit to your business.

As you have seen, Revenue Management technique is a sum of historical analysis, budgets, analysis of competition and the expected demand. Every day, every month and every year is different, and is what makes the work very rewarding and enjoyable revenue.

I encourage you, if you have any questions, to contact me.

I am also open to partnerships and consultations.

Do not hesitate to contact me via linkedin and if you are a Spanish speaker, i encourage you to follow my hotel revenue management blog: *hotelrevenuemanager.es*

ABOUT THE AUTHOR

 **Gemma Hereter** is a Revenue & Marketing Manager in Spain. Having studied Tourism and Communications she works as Revenue Manager and as a business developer.

Extremely versatile, she has managed & leaded teams, increased sales in the companies she has worked for and helped building brand awareness.

She is open for Revenue Management, Marketing, Business Development and Entrepreneurship consultancies.

Printed by Amazon Italia Logistica S.r.l.
Torrazza Piemonte (TO), Italy

50517188R00067